A GUIDE FOR

MW00770567

LET'S MOVE TO EUROPE!

MICHAEL OWENS

PEPPERBACK

Copyright © 2023 by Michael Owens

All rights reserved.

No portion of this book may be reproduced in any form without written permission from the publisher or author, except as permitted by U.S. copyright law.

ISBN 978-1-958559-10-9

Pepperback Press, Inc.

PepperbackPress.com

LIMIT OF LIABILITY/DISCLAIMER OF WARRANTY: THE PUBLISHER AND AUTHOR HAVE USED THEIR BEST EFFORTS IN PREPARING THIS BOOK. THE PUBLISHER AND AUTHOR MAKE NO REPRESENTATIONS OR WARRANTIES WITH RESPECT TO THE ACCURACY OR COMPLETENESS OF THE CONTENTS OF THIS BOOK AND SPECIFICALLY DISCLAIM ANY IMPLIED WARRANTIES OF MERCHANTABILITY OR FITNESS FOR A PARTICULAR PURPOSE. THERE ARE NO WARRANTIES WHICH EXTEND BEYOND THE DESCRIPTIONS CONTAINED IN THIS PARAGRAPH. NO WARRANTY MAY BE CREATED OR EXTENDED BY SALES REPRESENTATIVES OR WRITTEN SALES MATERIALS. THE ACCURACY AND COMPLETENESS OF THE INFORMATION PROVIDED HEREIN AND THE OPINIONS STATED HEREIN ARE NOT GUARANTEED OR WARRANTED TO PRODUCE ANY PARTICULAR RESULTS, AND THE ADVICE AND STRATEGIES CONTAINED HEREIN MAY NOT BE SUITABLE FOR EVERY INDIVIDUAL. NEITHER THE PUBLISHER NOR AUTHOR SHALL BE LIABLE FOR ANY LOSS OF PROFIT OR ANY OTHER DAMAGES, INCLUDING BUT NOT LIMITED TO SPECIAL, INCIDENTAL, CONSEQUENTIAL, OR OTHER DAMAGES.

To my beautiful daughter:

Thanks for putting up with me.

TABLE OF CONTENTS

INTRODUCTION

At the height of the COVID pandemic in 2020, I moved to Spain. That, in its entirety, is my sole qualification for writing this book. It may be interesting to note that I am also a single mother by choice, a writer, a teacher, a self-diagnosed Crazy Dog Lady, and the daughter of a librarian—but let's face it, my biggest accomplishment is simply that I did the thing and have lived to tell the tale. I think there are still people who are shocked by that fact.

I may be one of them.

Prior to moving to Spain, my longest move had been from Maryland to Virginia—about an hour's drive. I had, however, traveled quite a bit. One of the largest sources of stress that people discuss when moving internationally is travel with kids and pets. That, I was very good at. In 2012 I founded a dog rescue that has moved literally hundreds of dogs by air over the last decade.

Originally from Baltimore, Maryland, I moved to the Virginia suburbs of Washington, DC in my early twenties to work in the fledgling tech industry of the 90s. When I became burned out with tech a decade later, I put my master's degree in English to use as a teacher. When I became burned out with teaching, I went back to tech as a consultant. Somewhere in there I raised a kid and a whole bunch of dogs. I was approaching burnout again in tech when Covid hit. I was done. I was in my mid-40s and looking for a place to retire with my motley crew.

Thus begins our story...

THE HOW AND
THE WHY

Before I get into why we left, let me talk about why we could. It's important for me to acknowledge my privilege here. Not only did I have a good job, but I'm old enough that my college loans were reasonable. Because of that I was able to pay them off fairly early in my adult life. Entering adulthood without debt, I could save for and buy a house at twenty-five.

The money I would have otherwise been paying for rent was going into what is traditionally the safest gamble you can make. For most of history, real estate has been the chosen investment of the rich and their institutions. Just think, a bank is willing to lend large swaths of the population money to invest in real estate. They've run the numbers and they know a good deal when they see one. The appreciation and tax advantages of real estate are excellent—and even if you end up defaulting down the line, they can sell the property to offset any loss.

So all of that is to say that I started out in a very good position to be able to emigrate from the United States. My property had appreciated in value as I paid down the principal on my loan. Even the part of my monthly payment that didn't go toward lowering my loan, helped offset my taxes—so still a win.

One of the biggest flaws in the current trajectory of the US today is that homeownership is becoming completely out of reach for the average American. As the older generation crows over their huge real estate wins, they're missing the long term ramifications. If I were entering the housing market now, the home I lived in would be beyond my means. Home ownership costs have increased without accompanying increases in salary. That means that fewer young people are able to invest in their futures. The ones who are able to pull it off leave themselves with no safety net. Not only are they unable to support the industries that make up the economy because they have ZERO discretionary spending, they are also one missed paycheck away from disaster.

I don't want to live in a country where young families starting out have to throw away rent every month in apartments in areas that don't have access to open green spaces and fresh foods, and that are not safe for their children to play outside. I also don't want to live in a country where I and my neighbors don't have access to other basic human needs.

Yes, I'm talking about healthcare. If my house is burning down, I don't have to worry about comparison shopping fire departments or negotiating their prices. When I am having a health crisis, asking me to evaluate plans or doctors is not just ridiculous, it's cruel. I am an educated adult with four degrees and I don't understand American healthcare plans. I have been very lucky that I have had "good" health insurance for the majority of my life. Despite that, I have had to deal with exorbitant bills and lack of access to care. I have considered delaying life-saving surgery because no one could tell me how much it was actually going to cost me.

Living in a society where everyone has access to free healthcare changes how you view things. You don't realize how often you consider the costs of healthcare until you suddenly don't have to anymore.

As an immigrant in Spain, I pay for private insurance. This is, by far, the least expensive and highest quality policy I have ever been on. It covers 100% of the costs of my doctor and hospital care with no copay and no deductible. The cost is less than a third of my "good" policy through my employer in the US, which had ridiculously high copays and deductibles.

Another cornerstone of any successful society is education. As a former teacher with two master's degrees, I was appalled at the direction of education in the US. The coupling of real estate property taxes and education has long served as a way to maintain social hierarchy, whereby people who can afford to live in expensive homes get better education for their children. The increased funneling of tax dollars to private educational institutions serves the same purpose.

In case it isn't completely

obvious already, I did NOT vote for the 45th POTUS. But it wasn't his election that caused me to leave. No matter how trepidatious we all were right after the election, we were committed to the fight. My daughter and I marched—with half a million of our closest friends—in Washington and I ran for my local school board. I campaigned for local candidates and tried to raise awareness and organize resistance.

We had some wins, but in the background the Republican machine was churning out young, conservative judges with lifetime appointments at a horrifying rate. There were many people who tried to sound the alarm but for the most part, this judicial packing flew under the radar until it was way too late.

On September 18, 2020 the roof caved in, but the house had been on fire for years. Ruth Bader Ginsburg's death was the flame that ate away the curtains from the windows, but the room was already full of smoke. And I had already made my decision to leave months before.

Looking back I can't point to any one specific moment when I decided to leave the US. Even before the pandemic I was working remotely and had decided to leave the Washington, DC area. I was hoping to purchase a home in a more rural area where we could have more space. Through all of 2019 and even into the summer of 2020 I was still looking at—and making offers on—properties in the US. If we would have bought one of those houses, our lives would be very different right now.

But none of our offers were accepted and in the end, a property I'd once visited in Spain came available again. We made an offer and it was accepted. I'd flirted with the idea of moving to Spain for years so I had a good grasp of the steps involved. Suddenly that daydream was becoming reality. When the news broke that RGB had passed and the mad rush to install her replacement before the election came, I already had a foot out the door.

Today the Supreme Court of the United States is still the creature that the 2016 election made it. This once great institution is now just a pawn of the conservative oligarchy and will continue to erode the rights of Americans for decades to come.

If you've been dreaming of other places—better places—to retire, raise your children, or just live your life, the time is now.

Welcome to the next great migration. Grab your bags and check your ticket. This diaspora is about to leave the station.

WHY SPAIN?

I will start off by saying that if you are just beginning this process and you have no ties to any other country at the moment, Spain is an excellent choice. Until recently, the rules for immigration to Portugal were slightly easier, but both countries are gorgeous places with beaches and mountains and people who are welcoming to immigrants and largely speak English.

One of the most important rights to exercise as an American, is your right to travel the world. An American passport gives you opportunities that aren't available to many and it saddens me that so few Americans take advantage of those. While travel can be cost prohibitive at times, it isn't always. I've traveled round trip to Europe and back for less than it cost me for gas and tolls to the airport. Even in these days of volatile airline pricing, there are still great deals to be had if you keep your eyes—and your options—open.

Be flexible, see the world. It will change how you see yourself.

Not only had I traveled to Spain as a tourist in my 20s, I'd also traveled as a volunteer for animal rescue in the many (so many) years since then. In 2012 I adopted a Galgo Español, or Spanish Greyhound, named Josephine. Unlike the English Greyhounds who race in the US, the Galgo is primarily bred to hunt in the south of Spain. They race over the plains of Spain (where the rains, sadly, do not stay) and chase wild hare. At the end of the hunting season in February every year, tens of thousands of Galgos are abandoned or euthanized.

As a Greyhound owner for many years, I had volunteered with a local adoption agency and had a network of similarly dog-obsessed friends across North America. After adopting Josephine in 2012, I became deeply involved in Galgo rescue and founded a charity called The Sighthound Underground, dedicated to the welfare of Galgos, Greyhounds, and other Sighthounds around the world.

Because of my work with the dogs of Spain, I had the opportunity to travel there many times over the years and I was able to form opinions about the different regions. I knew where I wanted to be. I also was able to expand my network into Spain and had friends here that I could reach out to in an emergency. Although we didn't end up settling super close to any of our friends in the country, knowing that we had help an hour or two away was comforting. It also gave me a way to make adult friends pretty quickly. The south of Spain in particular has a thriving animal rescue community. There are opportunities to volunteer, fundraise, and socialize with other like-minded (and most often English-speaking) folks on a regular basis.

Besides my personal reasons for choosing Spain when I emigrated from the US, there are some objective statistics that make it a great choice. In addition to having excellent healthcare and education systems, Spain is also steeped in history and culture. Not only do many Spaniards speak English, but Spain is also a favorite tourist and retirement destination for English-speakers, most notably the British. Our local public highschool has one of the largest expat populations in Spain and nearly half of the student body are immigrants. Almost all of the immigrants in Spain speak English. My daughter, who arrived in Spain with basic Spanish, was fluent enough after a year to serve as a translator for students arriving from Ukraine who spoke English, but not Spanish.

The last huge plus in Spain's column is the weather. While there are areas in the north of Spain that are perfect for snow-lovers, we prefer the sunshine. Seasonal Affective Disorder (SAD) is very real and kept me from considering many locations. The sunshine in Spain is therapeutic.

On a personal note, the Mediterranean makes me happy. I don't even have to set foot on the beach. I can see it as I drive to the grocery store. That vast flat blue horizon catches my eye and I can't help but smile. I feel anchored and content. I was born and raised in Baltimore and lived my adult life in the Washington, DC suburbs of

Virginia, so I've always lived close to the Atlantic. It's a lovely ocean and I was always happy to see it. But the Mediterranean calls to me.

Even when the weather in Spain isn't perfect (I'm writing this as we finally surface from the rainiest Spring in recorded history) it is still gorgeous here. Gray days are few and far between. As soon as the rain clears the sun is rushing back onto the stage to put smiles (and freckles) on faces. We are near Alicante, which has recently been dubbed the sunniest city in Europe by Fodors. We have to agree.

It is important to remember that it hasn't always been sunshine and rainbows here. Spanish democracy was born from the death of Francisco Franco on November 20, 1975. From 1936, the country had languished under a fascist dictatorship that put them decades behind the rest of Europe in many ways. While there have been settlements in Spain for well over a million years–and the region has a rich history from the Romans to the Inquisition to the Spanish Civil War–the modern country of Spain is a child of the 70s and very much a member of Generation X.

The country, like its human cohort, is often overlooked both globally and even within Europe. This lack of visibility may in part be attributed to Spain's official neutrality during the two World Wars. When American GIs returned to their hometowns with stories of England, France, and Germany those countries grew to inhabit mythic standing in the American psyche. As a result, Spain has fewer than a third as many American immigrants as its neighbor, France.

In recent years, American immigration to Spain has started to increase and I hope that this book encourages that in some small part. Whatever country you choose when emigrating from the US, many of the steps will be the same. I hope that this account of my personal experience will at least give you a starting point to help you on your journey.

VIVA LA VISA
PART 1

All of this discussion of the whys and shoulds, is contingent on the can. Visit the website of your closest consulate for the country (or countries) you're interested in to see what visas they offer for long term and permanent residency. I'm going to discuss Spain (and Portugal somewhat), but every country has its own programs and requirements which are always changing and evolving. Generally, if you have an EU passport or can get one through a parent or grandparent, that is the easiest route to residency. In the US, there are special programs for those born in Puerto Rico (a former Spanish colony) as well.

If you have a sizable nest egg, this process can be much easier on you. Moving your savings or investments to Spanish banks or stocks can garner you a "golden" visa in as little as two weeks. There are many advantages to this type of visa, perhaps the most important being that you can apply directly from Spain and response times are usually speedy. In addition, the rules for renewal are much laxer as well. If you have $600,000 to spend on real estate or a couple of million in your retirement account, definitely contact a lawyer for more details.

The EU has been slowly phasing out these investment programs. The Portugal Golden Visa Program required a much lower investment and was very popular, but is scheduled to be terminated in 2023. Hopefully the program will be revived in the future. There have been discussions about ending Spain's program at some point as well, but for now it remains active.

Outside of an existing connection or a huge investment, visas have traditionally come in two main flavors–working or non-working. Working visas can be further divided into employee, self-employed, or entrepreneur. All of these require extensive documentation. It has been traditionally easier to get a non-working or non-lucrative visa because it meant you weren't taking away a job from a citizen of your chosen country. These were usually aimed at older immigrants and are known colloquially as "retirement" visas.

In recent years, a new version of the working visa has popped up in many countries specifically for remote workers. This year Spain has joined them in offering a so-called "Digital Nomad" visa. These visas are geared primarily toward IT and other professionals who can do their work online.

Had the "Digital Nomad" visa been an option in 2020, I might have considered applying. Many of us are lucky enough to be able to take our jobs with us. We can buy a home, a car, gas, food, etc. and contribute to the economy without taking a job from a Spanish citizen. Over the past 2-3 years Spain has struggled with understanding how this type of immigrant could fit into the existing visa structure. Since they didn't need permission to work for a Spanish employer, remote workers applied for the non-lucrative visa with great success for many years. Then the government clamped down and suddenly there was no path forward for those who wanted to continue to work their existing job from Spanish shores.

One of the weaknesses of Spanish bureaucracy can be its lack of flexibility. While other countries were able to roll out their Digital Nomad visas relatively quickly in response to the changing structure of modern online work, Spain responded by clamping down on the non-lucrative visa. Some people were asked to provide proof that they weren't working, including copies of letters of resignation, before being approved for their visas. To make matters even more frustrating, the policies varied from one consulate to another.

Spain has been tackling the lack of consistency between consulates over the last couple of years. In the past, visa requirements for Americans were specific to the consulate assigned to your state. If you were a resident of Florida, the process was smooth and the staff flexible. If you were applying through the Houston consulate, on the other hand...good luck. The rules were unclear and changed by the moment. At times applicants were told they couldn't hold a mortgage on a US property, that they had to produce a copy of the resignation letter from their US job, and proof that they had prepaid for a year's rent in Spain—all before receiving permission to make the move. These days the requirements are a bit more reasonable!

There are several main components for the Non-Lucrative Visa (NLV) in Spain and they are similar for most countries. The most important criteria is proof that you have the means to live in the country without needing to work. This is where Portugal has a distinct advantage. Their financial requirements are much lower than Spain's—in fact, at around $7500 they are less than a quarter Spain's requirement of over $30000. The amounts vary periodically, but they are generally in those ranges and have been for years. The good news is that you have several ways to reach those numbers.

Whichever country you're looking at, the financial requirements are annual. For your first year that means you can demonstrate the amount in savings, (passive) income, or a combination of both. And yes, ALL savings counts, such as money in 401Ks and trusts; and ALL passive income counts, including things like pensions, stock dividends, SSI, and disability payments. The complication can come when you renew your visa after the first

year. In Spain, the second renewal is for two years. If you've used passive income then you have no issues. You can include the same proof of that income. However, until recently if you used savings, then you needed to show double the amount to prove that you can support yourself for two more years. This tripped up many visa holders. Luckily, the government has addressed the issue and the "double requirement" is no longer being enforced in most areas.

As an aside, many NLV holders in Spain do transition to work visas. It is difficult to come to the country on a work visa because you need to have a job already in place. This can be very complicated to accomplish remotely. Spaniards, generally, have a strong preference for doing business face to face. It is much easier to find a job here once you've arrived, settled in, and had a chance to build connections in the community. Likewise, transition from the NLV to a working visa (or self-employed or entrepreneur visa) seems to be an easier process, from anecdotal evidence.

Whichever path you take to attain your first visa, the result is a full page sticker in your passport. You have 90 days to enter the country officially for the first time with the visa.

Then the real paperwork begins!

THE PAPERWORK
COMETH

For the vast majority of Americans, the first step in the visa process must take place in the US. It can take three to six months from start to finish and the longest delay is likely waiting for your documents to be authenticated.

Generally, there are two to four official government documents you will need to submit with your visa application. First, all applicants must provide a copy of their passport, and present the original when submitting the application. The second applies to all adult applicants and it is a criminal background report. Depending on your assigned consulate, if you have lived in your current state for at least five years, you may be able to submit a background report from your state police. If not, you'll need to go through the FBI, which can take a bit longer

to authenticate. If you're bringing children with you, you will need to provide a new copy of their birth certificate. This is an official copy of the birth certificate dated within three months. In Virginia I was able to go to our local DMV office to get this immediately. If you're married, you'll need to do the same thing with your marriage certificate. They will not accept the originals for either of these documents.

Here comes the part that trips up many applicants and causes delays, especially during the pandemic. Birth and marriage certificates, as well as the background report, must be authenticated by the issuing entity. So if your child was born in Virginia and has a birth certificate issued by the Commonwealth of Virginia, then once you have the new official copy in hand you will need to actually send that physical document back to the state to have an embossed seal affixed to it. This is an insane process and can take many weeks, and often months, to complete. For example, if you were married in Las Vegas, you're going to have to request a copy of your marriage certificate from Nevada and when it arrives, send it right back to Nevada to be authenticated.

Keep in mind that these documents are only good for three months. For those who have had to request an FBI background check, that document has to be authenticated by the US State Department. During the pandemic there were delays of up to three months, which meant that by the time you received your documents back, they were already out of date as far as Spain was concerned.

The seal of authentication that these government entities provide is called an apostille (uh-poss-ull) and consists of a sheet of paper with the certification in the form of a physical seal attached to the original document with a staple. DO NOT remove the staple. If you remove the staple to scan or email the docs, they become invalid and you have to start the process all over again. To scan or copy these documents, simply fold them back along the edge of the staple very, very carefully.

There are many companies that specialize in expediting these documents for you, but the costs vary greatly. In addition, in many cases you will still end up having to do a lot of the legwork. At the end of the day, wading through this bureaucratic minefield is good practice for your future life in Spain.

The next most complicated document you'll need is a health certificate. This has confused and frustrated many applicants because there are not clear parameters of the embassy's expectations. You can not just go to your doctor and request a health certificate. Not only will they have no idea what you're talking about, but it may also raise a red flag with them that you're looking for something they can't provide. Any reputable medical professional may balk at attesting that you are completely healthy and open themselves up to liability from you or your insurance company in the future.

Luckily, this is not what is required.

There are several examples of the language needed in the health certificate floating around the internet. Below is the one we used. While you will need to have many of your documents translated before you submit your application, any document you can provide natively in Spanish is preferred. Here is an opportunity to do so. I printed the English and Spanish versions of this text on a single sheet of paper and also emailed it to my doctor. It needs to be printed on their letterhead before being signed.

My primary care physician was willing to sign this document (twice, actually, since our first one expired), but I have heard many stories of people turned away by their doctors who where spooked by even this language. If

---

MEDICAL CERTIFICATE OF GOOD HEALTH

This certificate verifies that Mr./Ms. ....
.... is free of drug addiction, mental illness, and does not suffer from any disease that could cause serious repercussions to public health according to the specifications of the International Health Regulations of 2005. These contagious diseases include, but are not limited to smallpox, poliomielitis by wild polio virus, the human influenza caused by a new subtype of virus and the severe acute respiratory syndrome (SARS), cholera, pneumonic plague, Yellow fever, viral hemorrhagic fevers (e.g.: Ebola, Lassa, Marbug), West Nile Virus and other illnesses of special importance nationally or regionally (e.g.: Dengue Fever, Rift Valley Fever, and meningococcal disease).

Mr./Ms. .... is a very healthy individual in all senses, he/she has no pre-existing medical conditions, and she/he is capable of traveling abroad.

Por el presente se certifica que el Sr./Sra. ....
.... No padece ninguna drogodependencia, enfermedad mental o alguna de las enfermedades que suponen riesgo para la salud pública de conformidad con lo dispuesto en el Reglamento Sanitario Internacional de 2005. Estas enfermedades incluyen, entre otras, la viruela, poliomielitis por poliovirus, gripe humana causada por nuevos subtipos de virus, síndrome respiratorio agudo severo (SARS), cólera, neumonía, fiebre amarilla, las fiebres hemorrágicas virales (como el Ébola, Lassa, Marburgo, etc.), la fiebre del Nilo Occidental y otras enfermedades de ámbito nacional o regional (como el Dengue, fiebre del Valle del Rift, síndrome meningocócico, etc.)

El Sr./Sra. .... Se encuentra en buen estado de salud general y presenta un historial médico libre de enfermedades, por lo que se estima apto para viajar al extranjero.

---

you find yourself in that situation, your next option is to go to an urgent care clinic and ask to have it signed there. Be sure to show them the form at the desk and have the doctor take a look before you pay for the appointment. You may need to try a couple, but this has worked for everyone that I've spoken to.

The next set of documents will be your proof of financial resources. Many financial organizations these days have a place on their website that you can automatically request a "balance letter". You can also use regular bank statements, although those oddly formatted blank pages may add up when you go to get them translated. I submitted three months of statements for my regular accounts and my most recent quarterly statement for my retirement accounts. I've heard of people submitting as much as a year's worth of statements.

When it comes to financial documents, the closer you are to the minimum, the more documentation you may need to submit. There are anecdotal reports of applicants pooling their money to apply one at a time. Showing that the money has been in the account as long as you can is ideal. Also, if the money in your account came from one specific event, such as an inheritance or the sale of your house, providing that

NOTE!
Don't be afraid to negotiate with your translator. They will absolutely charge you for translating a page that says "This page is blank" if you let them.

documentation may help your case as well.

If you can't obtain your financial documents in Spanish, then these will also need to be translated, along with the apostilled government documents. On the embassy website there is a list of translators certified by Spain and you must use a translator from that list. The cost of translation varies and is usually calculated by the page. You will need every page of the certificates, including the apostilles themselves, as well as every page of bank statements translated. If the statement has a page number in the corner that includes a total number of pages, you'll need to provide all pages.

While you're waiting for your translations, which can take a couple of days to a week, it's time to request health insurance quotes. There are a handful of large insurance companies in Spain and they all seem to provide excellent service compared to what we're used to in the US. My advice is to look at the hospitals in the area you're interested in moving to and check their websites to see which companies they work with. Our closest hospital is in the Quirónsalud network and they seem to accept most insurances. I strongly recommend getting a couple of quotes. For myself and my daughter we received quotes ranging from 1000-1500€ a year. Since all "visa" policies must include a (very high) standard level of care, you will in most cases be comparing apples to apples.

Private health insurance policies in Spain will work in a similar way to what you're used to in the US. The main difference is that you will have access to the public healthcare system for some things like vaccinations. This is a change that happened during the pandemic. Previously immigrants with private insurance policies had little to no interaction with the public system. During COVID, anyone registered with their local town hall was able to go to the community clinic and register with the public health insurance system and get a temporary public health insurance ID (SIP) card. Initially this enabled them to qualify for COVID vaccines and boosters. In some regions those with the new SIP cards were also offered flu and tetanus shots.

The good news is that, overall, healthcare in Spain is excellent. Your new policy has no deductible and no copay. While it doesn't generally cover medications or dental care, those are both much, much less expensive in Spain. The bad news is that you will need to show proof that you have prepaid your policy for a year when you submit your application. That means that you will most likely be paying for at least a month if not two of insurance in Spain before you can enter the country.

Once you have paid for your policy, the company should send you a certificate to include with your visa application. By this point you hopefully have translations of your financial statements and apostilled certificates and background check in hand. The last documents you'll need are the official visa application form and the fee payment form. You can download these from the embassy website. Bring extra blank copies, just in case.

There is a fee for submitting your application, and it changes often. Like most administrative fees in Spain, it is calculated by some arcane math that yields odd numbers. Ask your embassy if they prefer a check, money order, or cash and come prepared.

THE MOMENT
OF TRUTH

Before your actual visa appointment, you will most likely need to scan and email all of your documentation to the consulate. Again, each location's requirements vary and you can't choose which one you have to deal with. The decision is based on your location. You'll need to visit the Spanish government website to figure out which consulate is yours.

Traditionally, Miami and DC have been the easiest to work with. Houston and Los Angeles the hardest. But keep in mind that the rules are subject to change and you need to be flexible throughout this process. The steps below are general and your experience may vary.

The email that you send to the consulate should include one PDF with all of your documents neatly organized. The first page should be a brief cover letter with a happy little note—in Spanish, scanned in with an ink signature—stating why you are obtaining the visa. This letter should be short and positive. Don't provide unnecessary information. On the following page is an example of what we used.

The next page in your PDF file will be a table of contents or simple list of the documents included in your file. It should look something like this:

1. Application Form
2. Fee Payment Form
3. ID Page of your Passport
4. Driver's License
5. A Passport sized photo of yourself
6. Medical Certificate
7. Healthcare Policy Cert
8. Healthcare Policy Receipt

Dear Sir or Madam:

I am writing this letter in support of my family's application for a one-year non-lucrative visa to reside in Spain. My family and I have visited Spain many times and have many friends there. We are excited by the opportunity to spend a year living in the country to which we have so many emotional bonds.

I have attached financial records showing that we have sufficient funds to support our needs. We hope these documents will help to establish our financial responsibility and solvency. We also hope that our letters of clearance from our doctor and my background check document will demonstrate our good character and health.

9. Background Check
10. Financial Statement(s)
11. Marriage Certificate (if applicable)
12. Rental Contract (if required)

Even if you don't have a rental contract, you'll need to provide an address for where you'll be staying when you arrive in Spain. You can also use a friend's address. Keep in mind that the final approval of your application is actually up to the individual Autonomous Community you will be residing in, so this matters. If you plan to settle in Catalonia, don't put down an address in Murcia.

Each person in your family will need to have all of the applicable documents. Children don't need to have background checks, or driver's licenses, but they do need to each have their own application form and medical certificate, for example. You will have an insurance certificate for each person, but proof of payment only for the main applicant.

Each dependent will have:

1. Application Form
2. ID Page of your Passport
3. A Passport sized photo
4. Medical Certification
5. Healthcare Policy Cert
6. Healthcare Policy Receipt
7. Background Check (if over 18) or Birth Certificate (if under 18)

Once you have scanned all of these documents and emailed them to the consulate, they should reply with further instructions. In many cases it will be an in person appointment to submit the documents. During the pandemic, some consulates were having applicants mail all of the original documents in, but it seems like that has ended at this point. Again, pay attention and be flexible. Things can change without warning and you need to always be responsive and polite when dealing with consulate staff.

In our case, we received appointments about a month away. You will need an official appointment for each person—even infants—but in practice they will take you all at once. On the day of your appointment, bring all of your original documents and a full copy for each person in your party as well as a labeled and prepaid priority mail envelope. Be prepared to leave your passports with the consulate.

During the appointment, there is no "interview" per se. At the consulate in DC, you will stand at a window, like in a bank. You will slide your documents under the glass to the staff member and they will review each one, placing them in piles. They will hand back to you anything they don't need and will request anything missing. Don't panic. In some cases you will be allowed to mail in any missing documents. In our case I had made a mistake on our application form and they provided me with a blank copy and walked me through filling it out correctly.

We were told we could bring

a cashier's check or cash for the application fee. Since I'd heard different things about the fee and the way it's calculated can be somewhat convoluted, I just brought cash (with plenty of small bills to make change).

The last question the consulate staff may ask you is your date of arrival in Spain. The visa that they issue and affix to your passport is only good for three months. Once you arrive in Spain there will be further steps—that we will discuss in the next chapter—to convert that into a one year residency. But you must enter Spain (legally, through customs) before that three month expires.

At the end of the interview, leaving the consulate is somewhat anticlimactic. There is an immediate sense of relief at having handed in your documents, but you're still in limbo. Make sure to keep the tracking number for the prepaid envelope you've left with the consulate. Try to only check the number once or twice a day. The consulate should give you a time estimate. In our case they told us three weeks, and we received our passports back with their shiny new visas attached in exactly two weeks.

While you're waiting, be sure to stop by your local AAA office to get your International Driver's Permit.

You're getting close.

PREPARING TO MOVE A LIFETIME OF CRAP

With a history of one of the most difficult consulates to work with, Houston has in the past put in place stringent requirements that are unique to that location. The most onerous of these was their insistence that Americans cannot apply for a visa if they are currently paying a mortgage on property in the US. This requirement was absolutely ridiculous and put an end to many people's dreams of emigration. If you had been denied a visa for this reason, your only option was to sell your home or establish residency in a different state to apply again through another consulate.

Luckily the move toward standardization of the visa process across consulates has alleviated most of these absurd demands, but selling your home at some point in the process is a hurdle many applicants may face regardless. The decision as to when or whether to sell your home in the US is not an easy one. It will depend on your financial resources and will greatly impact the logistics of your move. In our case, we were able to go directly from our home in the US to our rental in Spain with no temporary housing needed in between. Since we were traveling with pets, that was crucial.

There is one basic consideration you need to make when preparing for an international move. Are you having your belongings shipped? If not, then your next step is easy. Pack the things you need–personal effects, documents, mementos, your clothing and valuables into XL Heavy Duty boxes and bring them with you on your flight. When we checked in I was pleasantly surprised to be told that Iberia offers free additional baggage allowance to passengers flying on new residency visas. That was a lovely bonus. I brought two suitcases and 3 XL boxes on my flight. These were my "must have" items.

I also decided to have the rest of my belongings shipped. I have vacillated over this decision. Do I regret it? Sometimes. Am I glad I did it? Usually. The bottom line is that almost anything you are thinking of shipping to Spain is going to be available here locally, and most likely for much less. Was it necessary to have my household goods shipped? No. Was I so happy to see my own ratty old couch that I cried a little? Also yes.

In theory, I could have sold everything that I owned and purchased new in Spain and probably come out ahead and saved myself the cost (and headache) of shipping. But in practice, I didn't have the time or energy to sell everything before leaving and buying everything new on arrival would have been a nightmare.

The day the shippers came to collect our things was absolutely chaotic. The movers swept through the house like locusts, leaving disaster in their wake. Many items that I loved ended up being left behind and I just gave them away. It was traumatic and not a great experience. But a month later, when I saw that big metal container again and the doors swung open, I was nearly giddy with happiness.

If you decide to ship your belongings, there are three pieces of advice I would give. First, comparison shop and negotiate. Speak to several companies and make your choice based on recommendations and ask them to match the lowest quote you receive. I went with the lowest quote and after the fact found out that my first choice company would have matched it. I have regret. The shipping company that I went with told me not to pack beforehand. They said that the movers needed to pack every box to create a manifest and doing it ahead of time was just a waste of effort. That was a lie. I had packed about half of my boxes before I was told this and those boxes went right onto the truck. They were not opened and inspected and repacked. Those boxes were the only ones properly packed.

So my first piece of advice: Pack your own boxes.

Organize the belongings you're going to take. I would put them together in a room or two and make it very clear what is going and what isn't. I had marked items not going with bright neon post-it notes. Small appliances like microwaves and corded electric tools are not compatible with the voltage in Spain. They don't just require an adapter, they need an expensive inverter to function. In most cases, it's just not worth it. As you may have guessed, all of these items were in the boxes I unpacked in Spain. I had to leave my grandfather's great aunt's antique cream leather-topped lady's oval writing desk and matching chair because the movers said they didn't have room. My $10 electric egg steamer was wrapped in 10lbs of packing paper in an XL box with the bright pink post-it note saying "Do NOT pack" still attached.

The last thing you should know before shipping your belongings is that you will need extensive paperwork to receive your delivery on the other side. Spanish customs has the right to hold your items indefinitely. If you do not provide the paperwork they are looking for, they will go through your belongings one by one and assign a value and then charge you a rather large percentage of that value in order to have your items released.

In my case, the documents I needed to receive my shipment unmolested were a copy of my visa application, a copy of my taxes for the previous year showing a US address, a copy of the purchase contract of my house in the US from 12 years previously and a copy of the sales contract for the same house dated that month, and the magic document...the Baja Consular.

The Baja Consular is literally just a handwritten (in Spanish) document that you have witnessed at an American consulate in Spain stating that you have lived in the US and now you are going to live in Spain. It's silly and—if your home in Spain is not close to a US consulate—it's inconvenient. But it does for some reason make the Spanish customs agents very happy. And when your customs agent is happy, you are happy.

Appointments at the US consulates in Spain can be hard to come by, so this is something you may want to schedule ahead of time to take place in the first days after your arrival. Even with a short wait, I was in and out of the office within fifteen minutes-which almost made up for the two hour drive to get there.

TRAVELING WITH PETS

I moved to Spain with eight dogs. When I get to that part of the story, people are often amazed and astonished that I was able to pull off such a feat. In reality, that was one of the easiest components of our move. As the Director of an international rescue, I have traveled with multiple dogs on many occasions and have arranged the logistics for other volunteers to do so as well. Granted, those trips were all in the opposite direction, but the basic components of international travel with dogs are the same.

The very first thing you need to do when you have made the decision to move is arrange for all of your pets to see the vet. They will all need their microchips and vaccinations checked out. This is also a good time to do a general health inventory and get some bloodwork done so that you have a baseline for your new vet when you arrive in Spain.

More on this later, but for the record, veterinary care in Spain is affordable and excellent. Just like in the US, there are small, independent clinics with one or two doctors, chains with rotating staff, and large veterinary hospitals with 24 hour care. The quality of the veterinary care we have received in Spain is equal to or superior to the US and the

NOTE!

From the airline's point of view, 8 seems to be the magic number. For Spanish customs, it's 10. If you need to travel with more pets, plan on 2 trips.

cost is half to even a quarter or less. In addition, vets in Spain use most of the same medications, the bloodwork uses the same values, etc. The continuity of vetcare moving from the US to Spain is smooth.

In preparation for your trip, your pets will need at least one more vet visit. For this visit, make sure ahead of time that your veterinarian is certified with the USDA to prepare international import permits. Not every vet is. At this visit the vet will once again test your pet's microchip and go over their vaccine information. All of this info will be entered into the USDA system electronically. The USDA will then mail you a physical Spanish import permit. If you have five or fewer pets, this form will be good for ten days. If you have six to ten pets, this permit is only good for two days. If there are multiple people flying, you can split the pets onto multiple permits, one for each person.

The USDA system is not available on the weekends, so if you have more than five pets you will not be able to fly on a Monday morning to Spain–a lesson I found out the hard way.

Since the pandemic there are fewer non-stop flights to Europe from the US and many airlines have made the decision to stop carrying pets. If at all possible, avoid flights with layovers or connections. If there are going to be problems, that's where they occur 99% of the time.

For most of my travel to and from Spain, I have been on Iberia. It's been over ten years since my first flight with a dog on Iberia and on that flight the employee at the desk laughed when we told her we were bringing home Spanish Galgos. She couldn't understand why we would want them. Over the years there has been a slow and steady change in the attitude of the airline's employees (and the rest of the Spanish population) and the desk staff are much more welcoming these days. This is indicative of the changes in Spanish society as a whole, which has evolved tremendously in its attitudes toward animals, especially dogs, in the last decade.

The last element of your dogs' flight preparation is their crate. If you have a large breed dog, make sure to leave yourself enough time to buy, borrow, or steal a varikennel 700 size crate. These are not easy to come by and are (as I write this) not being made due to a manufacturing issue. If you are flying together, this size crate will work for even the largest dog. If you're sending your dog alone on a flight as cargo, then there are different rules and you may need to pay to have a wood crate fabricated for your pet.

For the dog, flying as

"checked baggage" with their person or flying as "cargo" on a plane alone, is exactly the same experience. You will check them in and they will be taken to the plane and ride in the hold. After landing they will be brought to the terminal or cargo office where you will meet them. The difference to you, however, can be quite important. For one thing, flying with your dog is about a tenth the cost of flying separately. For example, the cost to fly with a dog in the hold on Iberia has recently increased from 300€ to 360€. To fly them separately as cargo can be anywhere from 2000-5000€. In addition, when dogs are flown as cargo they must adhere to more stringent requirements for both their documentation and their crates. Dogs flying cargo must have extra clearance for both height and length that often sizes them out of the commercially available crates.

The bottom line is that it is always better to fly with your dogs if at all possible. For our trip, we were flying on a Monday. Luckily there were two of us so we split our dogs into two groups, each with its own import permit valid for ten days. We were leaving from Virginia but chose to fly out of New York on a direct flight to Madrid. We had friends in the US drive us to JFK airport in New York City and friends in Spain, who are certified pet transporters, pick us up in Madrid and drive us down to our rental house in Alicante.

In New York, we presented ourselves at the check-in desk with luggage, leashed dogs, and assembled crates. The airline staff gave our paperwork a cursory glance and handed over a stack of forms to fill out for each dog. As each form was completed, the dog was put into the crate and stickers affixed to the exterior. I ziptied all four corners of each crate and the four corners of each door. Porters took the dogs to the plane in ones and twos. When the dogs were all checked in, we handed over our luggage and headed for our gate.

Eight hours later, we deplaned in Madrid and had our passports stamped at border control. In the luggage area, our grouping of very large crates was easy to find. Once we were all together, the porters walked us over to a window where our USDA import permits were closely examined. We had to take out each dog and the staff scanned their chip and examined their paperwork. It seemed like a lifetime but it was probably no more than 30 minutes and we were on our way.

Google tells me that the drive from the airport in Madrid to our rental house in Alicante should have taken a little more than four hours, but it took us over six. We made several pit stops—including one for dog food—along the way. When we arrived at our rental house, we were all exhausted. Luckily it was still light out so I was able to walk the fence line and note the weak areas. We reinforced them with some handy bungee cords and let the dogs explore. Two immediately shimmied through the fence (and into another fenced area, thankfully) so more work was needed. By dark the fence was deemed secure and our dogs enjoyed a welcome little run before bed...during which one of them fell into the pool. At least we can say our life in Spain began with a splash!

A PLACE TO HANG YOUR HAT PART 1

There are many things that America doesn't do well. Healthcare, gender equality, LGBTQ rights. The one area where the US does have an advantage over Spain and many other places? Regulation of the construction and sale of residential real estate.

Who knew, right?

In most places in the US you can look up the history of any property you're interested in buying, including its owners and the prices they paid. When submitting an offer to purchase a home you can look up the record of building permits issued to the property, hire experienced home inspectors to check the electrical, HVAC, and plumbing systems, and even purchase title insurance.

When it comes to real estate, Spain is the wild west. The building codes like the ones that we take for granted in the US are a fairly new development in Spain. Even worse, real estate agents have been completely unregulated here until recently. It is important to know that there is no such thing as a buyer's agent—although there is nothing to stop agents from presenting themselves as such. There is also no board of ethics, and very little recourse when a real estate agent "takes the money and runs".

The good news is that there is a growing awareness of this issue and an effort to bring Spain up to the standards of the rest of Europe. As of October of 2023, agents operating physical locations in Valencia will have to register with the province. Registration requires a minimal amount of training and insurance, so that's a step in the right direction.

Regardless, whether you're intending to rent for a while or buying a house immediately, you must operate with the utmost caution. If you're buying an apartment in a large metropolitan area, the risks may be less than those looking for a single family home, especially in a rural area.

In Spain there are two main types of properties. Urbanizations are towns or cities where land has been designated for residential development. Those in urbanizations have some regulation and there are standards in place and they are more likely to be enforced. The town hall of each urbanization will be watching, to varying extents. Rural, or rustic, properties are outside of the designated areas of development. These properties have much less oversight and present a much greater challenge to the unsuspecting buyer or renter.

Another issue you may have as a renter is acquiring the landlord's permission to register as a resident of the property with the local town hall–and you will need a copy of this registration, referred to as a *certificado de empadronamiento or padrón* (pah-droan), to finalize your visa within 30 days of your arrival in Spain.

If the landlord is reluctant to provide you with documentation for the *padrón*, that can be a sign that the unit is not a legal rental.

Remember that you will need a signed copy of the lease or a signed letter from the property owner and documentation of their ownership of the property. If you're purchasing a property, the purchase contract and a signed letter from the owner granting permission for you to be added to the *padrón* for the property may suffice.

When it comes to renting, there are some protections for renters–but only if you know about them and are able to advocate on your own behalf. Remember that realtors are unregulated and not bound to any ethical standards and consult an actual attorney.

Note: In any real estate transaction, it is highly recommended to use an *independent* attorney to review all contracts. Generally, it is better to find your own attorney through references than to use the one who regularly partners with the real estate agent.

Some of the protections for renters in Spain include rent increase controls and extensive eviction protections as well as advantages in lease terminations. Although it is very difficult to be legally evicted, renters have the right to terminate a lease after 6 months for any reason.

One of the common scams in Spain is from real estate agents who demand as much as a month's rent as a fee from both landlord and tenant. In addition, deposits are rarely returned, so plan ahead when paying your final month's rent.

Housing costs in Spain are relatively inexpensive compared to most places in the US, but beware the hidden fees and taxes. Landlords can legally only charge one month's rent deposit and first month's rent upfront, but many will try to negotiate for more. On top of that the agent may try to take another month's rent. These extra costs add up quickly. If you're buying, you'll find a myriad of hidden fees, as well as a hefty sales tax of 8-10%. If the home you're buying isn't in compliance with the town hall, there may be additional fees to pay there as well. While there are mortgages available in Spain—even to non-residents—expect to put up 20-30% of the purchase price as a deposit plus another 12-15% in closing costs.

Sales contracts in Spain are typically in two parts. An initial offer may include a token deposit, usually 1000-3000 euros. This is a very brief document that simply identifies the parties and indicates the buyer's interest in the property and the offer price. Once that document has been accepted, a much more detailed contract will be drafted and a larger deposit placed on the property. It is important to make sure that language is included in both contracts that makes clear who is responsible for paying the costs associated with bringing the property into compliance with the local town hall.

As I mentioned previously, there is not as much public data available in Spain as there is in most areas of the US. In fact, you may not even be allowed to know the address of the property until you are ready to make an offer, due to the strict privacy laws. In three years I have never seen an open house here. The best places to start your search for property is going to be online or at your local realtor's office. Once you've landed, drive through the neighborhoods you're interested in to look for "*Se Vende*" signs. You can contact most of the numbers on WhatsApp.

When you're looking online, be prepared to look past bad pictures. Staging homes is not a common practice in Spain and many of the houses you'll see will be full of not just the current occupant's belongings—but also in many cases piles of trash. Especially if you're looking at a rural home, you may need to do some major cleanup upon possession. Even in urban areas, it is not unusual for sellers to leave furniture and other items. On the other hand, it is also common for them to take large kitchen appliances. Your new home may have three couches and no refrigerator upon move-in. Ours did!

Since we were waiting for our container to arrive from the US, we were grateful for the furniture left behind. If you don't need the items—or when you're ready to get rid of them—there are usually a myriad of charity shops who are willing to pick up the pieces. Likewise, if you find yourself with three couches and no beds, the charity shops are a good place to fill any gaps.

A PLACE TO HANG YOUR HAT PART 2

Once you've found a place to live, you'll soon notice some differences to what you're used to in the US. Some of these changes you'll get used to rather quickly. For example, the large AC or heat pump units we're used to in most of the US aren't common in Europe. Here mini splits are the HVAC unit of choice. In recent years these small, practical units have been becoming more popular in the US, as well, so you may be familiar with them already. If not, you'll soon find them an easy to use and energy efficient option.

Even in homes with robust HVAC systems, you'll find windows open during the mild parts of the day. This is healthy practice and reflected in the architecture, which often includes metal bars on windows, security doors, and walled gardens. These allow residents to leave their windows open without risking an invitation to petty theft. Although Spain is a very safe country, theft can be an issue and security systems are strongly recommended.

Surprisingly, window screens are not common. Even newer houses may not have insect screens installed and having them retrofitted can be surprisingly expensive. Higher end windows may have screens that roll up, which I've never seen in the US. These are convenient, but they do have some downsides. First, they're not patchable and are very expensive to replace if damaged. Second, they don't make a tight seal against the window sill and the edges can let in the odd fly or two.

Along with the roll up screens, windows here often feature

exterior rolling metal shutters. In the heat of the summer day, being able to completely close off the windows can have a major impact on the interior temperature of your home and at night, they give you complete privacy. The only downside to the rolling shutters is that they do leave the exterior of the home or building looking very plain and unlived in. The main street of our small town looks deserted in the evenings when the blinds are all down.

The home we purchased in Spain is actually outside of the town, in the rural area, often referred to as rustic land. Not only are we beyond the limits of the urbanization, but we're about a mile down a private road. There are very few lights at night and we've found that the GPS directions can go astray here.

Living in the countryside, or "el campo", we do not have trash pickup. Instead we have to throw our trash into the car and drive it to one of the many collection points in town. Every street (in some cases, every block) in the urbanization has its own small, covered dumpster. Many times these are divided into recycling stations. They're usually very clean and neat and often have a foot pedal to open the lid, for hands-free access. The units are emptied once a day via a cute little garbage truck with a mechanical

arm. The downside to this type of trash pickup is that people will often leave excess or oversize items beside the bins and those can not be picked up automatically. In most places, you can call the number on the side of the bins or the local town hall to arrange a special pick up for those items.

Just like in the US, if you set something useful by the side of the road, it may be picked up quickly. Facebook marketplace is also very active in our area and we've scored some great free or cheap furniture pieces to help us set up our new home. If you're looking for new pieces, there is every level of furniture available here, from high end stores to IKEA.

MONEY IN SPAIN

One of the very first things you need to do once you have arrived—or even beforehand—is open a bank account. You do not need to wait until you have residency to open an account, and having one in place will make the details a lot easier as you go about setting up the other elements of your life here.

Periodic bills—your telephone, mobile, internet, water, electric, security system monitoring, etc.—will be paid by automatic debit from your bank account. In most cases this bank account must have a Spanish IBAN identifier. At the writing of this book, it appears that of the online banks, only N26 offers a Spanish IBAN with their accounts. Having a local bank can come in handy, however. Taxes and municipal fees (Suma) can be paid at your local branch (as well as online) and you'll need to be able to withdraw euros so that you have cash on hand. Keep in mind that you will not be able to deposit dollars into your Spanish account and receive euros. The banks here do not do exchanges. You can, however, use a US bank card to take out euros at any ATM. If you have a Charles Schwab account, they reimburse all fees.

Opening a bank account in Spain can be almost as difficult as your original visa process. I have heard of people who walk into their local branch and walk out 10 mins later with an account. That is the exception. For the vast majority of us, opening a bank account in Spain is an adventure. In the past Spain has struggled with rampant money laundering. As a result there has been a heavy-handed crack down in the banking industry that has created a bureaucratic quagmire in many cases. Ironically, the burdensome paperwork and high taxes (VAT) have also resulted in a very cash-oriented society. Whether you're having your lawn mowed or your pool tiled, you will find vendors eager to deal in cash—and willing to offer you a significant discount to do so.

This is never a good idea. In addition to the penalties that may arbitrarily be handed down from the tax authority, money off the books means work off the books, which means your investment is not protected or warrantied. No matter how charming your builder seems, insist on paying through bank transfer and receiving an invoice and receipt.

In the past, even home sellers have tried to deal in "black money", a cash component of the sale that isn't recorded. While you may still need a cashier's check to bring to your closing when you buy a house, personal checks just aren't a thing in Spain. All transactions are done via cash or electronic transfer. There are several different types of transfers, and they each have their own fees and timelines.

The first step, whether you're dealing in electronic or cash money, is to set up your Spanish account so that you can turn your dollars to euros. When selecting a

bank, keep in mind that branches are set up as individual institutions in Spain. While you may be able to use any ATM in the network, if you move from one town to another, you'll most likely have to close your account and set up a new one, even if the banks are part of the same company.

When you arrive at the bank, you will need to bring three sets of documents with you. The first set is the easiest, and that is your proof of identity. Generally this will be your passport, which you should carry with you at all times until you recieve your Foreigner's Identification Card (TIE). The second set of documents is your proof of residency status. Banks have different types of accounts for different types of customers and it is not easy to move between them. For example, when I set up my first bank account in Spain, I had to set up a non-resident account, even though I already had my visa and was living in Spain. Because I did not have my physical TIE card yet (more on that later) I could not set up a resident account. When I received my first TIE, I switched the account—since the resident account had no fees. When it was time for me to renew my TIE card, that bank account was "locked" between the time my old card expired and the time I brought in my new card to be authenticated, which was several months. Interestingly, although they would not serve me at the counter, I was still able to use my ATM card to withdraw cash.

The third set of documents you will need to open an account is proof of the origin of your funds. This may also determine what kind of account you can open. For example, it is much easier—and you will have fewer fees—if you open an account that will receive a regular pension payment. If you're opening an account with a one-time lump sum, you'll need to show proof of where that money came from in the form of paystubs, taxes, house sale contracts, etc.

As with many things in Spain, you are at the mercy of the individual agent who is reviewing your documents. Be nice. Be patient. And be prepared to shop around if you don't like your options. Also, keep in mind that any change in your account will result in a change to the actual account number. Generally the bank will take responsibility for migrating your existing automatic payments.

VIVA LA VISA
PART 2

Once you arrive in Spain, the second part of the visa process begins. In many ways, these steps mirror what you've already gone through in the US. Be prepared to have all of the same paperwork, and then some.

The most important document that you'll need is your NIE (foreigner's ID number) certificate. This is a plain sheet of paper with your name and NIE number printed on it. This number is usually assigned to you when your visa is issued and you will also find it on the visa sticker in your passport. Some people do get an NIE earlier in the process. You can apply for one if you're thinking of buying property in Spain, or doing any kind of business. The NIE is basically your SSN for Spain.

You may wonder why you need the plain paper certificate if the number is already on your visa in your passport. There is no good answer to that question, except to say that you are in Spain now and you should pick your battles. We were able to get a copy of our NIE from our local town hall, but you also may need to go to your local foreigner's office for that.

The next document that you need is your padrón. This is a certificate of your registration with your local town hall. If you're renting when you first arrive, try to stay in the same locality that you intend to settle in. If you've already put an offer on a house, the seller may be willing to let you register at that address before the sale. You will only need your sales contract and a letter from them granting their permission.

The third and final document you need before your appointment to finalize your residency, is a tax receipt showing you have paid the fee for your TIE (foreigner's ID card). You actually pay this as part of the application fee for the visa itself in the US and the consulate should provide this document. However, the amount of this fee changes often and if it is not exactly the same as your receipt, you will need another one. The good news is that the fee is usually around 12€, so don't stress about having to pay it twice. As mentioned previously, this is one of those fees that you can pay in person at a bank, through your bank's app, or online.

Once you have gathered those three documents, plus all of the paperwork you took to your visa appointment (passport, birth certificates, photographs, etc.) as well as a complete set of copies of everything, you are ready for your TIE appointment at the foreigner's office. Keep in mind that you may have to travel fairly far afield to find an appointment. We traveled about an hour for our appointment.

These appointments are notoriously hard to get, especially post BREXIT. The only way to get an appointment is through the website and they are made available sporadically. There are many different strategies for "gaming the system" and some people do get lucky. The bottom line is that you are supposed to have this appointment within 30 days of your arrival in Spain. If you haven't been able to get an appointment, don't panic. This happens to many people. But do consider hiring a lawyer or a *gestor* to set the appointment for you.

Gestors are managers or "fixers" and are useful for many different activities in Spain. They can help with paperwork at the town hall or the foreigner's office, can serve as translators, and smooth the way as you adjust to life in Spain. There is, however, a huge spectrum of both fees and levels of service associated with *gestors*. One *gestor* may charge 10€ for a service and another may charge 50€. The differences can be extreme. Shop around and ask for references.

As an aside, every town and region in Spain has local groups on facebook—often many. You may find different groups for Spanish and English speaking residents. If your Spanish is not up to par, use Google Translate to join the Spanish-speaking groups. You will find the vendors recommended there much less expensive.

Once you have acquired your TIE appointment, the most important advice I can give is to bring everything. Even things that other people have said you do not need. Just get into the habit of bringing all of your paperwork to every Spanish appointment.

The foreigner's offices in Spain are all in National Police buildings. When you arrive—during the post-COVID era—there is a police officer sitting outside to direct traffic. For those with appointments, you are allowed into the building immediately. Once inside you may have to wait a bit until you are seen but generally the offices seem to run fairly smoothly.

Although you do need to make a separate appointment for each member of your family, when it is the first person's turn, you can usually approach the desk as a group, especially if you have children with you. But the staff member will look at the paperwork one person at a time. Part of the process is also taking fingerprints, which does not always go smoothly. It can take 3 or 4 tries to get a satisfactory print. Be patient and follow the agent's directions.

Some people may wish to bring a translator to this appointment. It is not usually necessary for several reasons. First of all, you can just hand over your documents so the need to communicate is minimal. Second, the agent will often speak at least serviceable English. Third, translators may not be allowed in the building. The same is true for lawyers or *gestors*.

At the end of your TIE appointment, you will receive a very important piece of paper with your *"lote"* number on it. TIE cards are printed in batches off-site and the *lote* number indicates what batch your card will be delivered with. When you leave this appointment you are basically finished with the visa and residency process (for now) but it will be another 4-6 weeks until you have your physical card.

Before you leave the police station, make sure to ask what number you should call to find out the current *lote* number. This will save you having to come in person to check, which may be quite a long drive. At about the four week mark, check in to see what *lote* your office is on. I've found it is best to call right at 9AM.

When your *lote* number comes up, most regions do not require you to make another appointment to pick up your card. You can show up any morning to the police station right at 9AM, but be prepared for a short wait. Generally they will only take people until 1PM or 2PM, so earlier is better.

The very important paper you received with your *lote* number is your ticket into the police station this time, although these days you will usually be asked to wait outside and brought inside in small groups. You will again wait to be called and come up to the same desk as the original appointment. You'll hand over your paper, show your passport, and then have to go through the fingerprinting process all over again. Once you have been able to produce a successful fingerprint, the agent hands you your precious card and you are on your way.

Your card is dated from the day that you arrived in Spain with your visa. If it takes you two months to receive your card, then you will only have 10 months until it expires. You can start the renewal process two months beforehand. Definitely do that. Keep in mind that you can not do many things without the physical card, even if your renewal has been approved.

DRIVING IN SPAIN
PART 1

As I write this, the fallout from BREXIT is still hitting British residents in Spain. Many of them have driven for years on their UK driver's licenses and many are just arriving. Both groups are shocked to realize that they are no longer able to simply exchange their licenses for the Spanish equivalents.

This option was never open to Americans. Within the US, each state has its own license with its own tests and policies. You can easily exchange your state license when you move from state to state. However, this state-based system prevents Americans from exchanging our licenses in Spain. Since there is no Federal level driver's license and Spain does not have reciprocal agreements with each of the individual states in the US, there is no exchange for Americans.

Upon your arrival in Spain, Americans are required to go through the entire driver's education and testing process from scratch, which is both expensive and difficult. While you can use an international driver's permit with your US license when you first arrive, once you have been in Spain for six months past the date on your TIE card, that permit is technically no longer valid. Since it can take a couple of months to get your TIE and it can take that long or longer to get through the driver's license process in Spain, it is important to start the process as soon as you receive your TIE card. Keep in mind that your car insurance company will have no problem with writing a policy for you after your International permit expires, but if you're in an accident they will most likely not honor it.

The standard license in Spain is a type "B", but just like in the US there are different licenses for things like big trucks and motorcycles. Although the age minimum for the standard license is 18 (to my teenager's dismay), Spain does offer licenses to drivers as young as 15. These are restricted to vehicles under 50cc, which include several styles of scooters and "microcars". Some of these options are quite cute and many older drivers consider them as well, since the written and practical tests are both much easier.

The first step in the process is to find a driving school, or *autoescuela*. This is not optional, unfortunately. While you can take the written test independently, you will need to sign up with a driving school for your practical exam. No matter how long you have been driving, you still must have at least one practical lesson at a Spanish school. You will need the school to actually register you for the test and you will be using their vehicle to take it.

It's very important to join local groups on facebook to gain access to a variety of information and social activities, etc. but the recommendations for tradesmen and local businesses like *autoescuelas* can be invaluable. I initially chose the school closest to my home—without checking references. This turned out to be a huge mistake. For one thing, you will be doing your practice lessons in the area of the actual test— which can be quite far. I spent literally half of each lesson driving on the highway to and from the test area. Even more importantly, my first instructor's English was not as fluent as advertised and he became extremely frustrated with me during our lessons. This was not helpful.

Before you get to the practical lessons, you must first pass a basic health screening and the written test. The health screening, or *psicotécnico*, consists of a cursory eye exam and a very basic hand-eye coordination test. I was pretty sure I had failed the test, but apparently the bar is quite low.

The same is not true, unfortunately, of the written test. Even in English, this test is incredibly difficult—and very different from what you may dimly remember from your teenage years. A large number of the test questions consist of scenarios and obscure traffic rules that— to Americans—seem needlessly complicated. Shall we discuss the double stop? In addition, some of the rules change based on the type of area (urban or rural), the type of vehicle, the time of day, etc. The pictures that accompany the scenarios often make the context even murkier.

Another difference in the Spanish written exam compared to US equivalents, is the focus on equipment. You will find a significant portion of the questions revolve around things like engine size and a vehicle's maximum velocity. There are pieces of equipment and specific documents that need to be kept in your vehicle and there are cycles of inspections that change based on various criteria. It's a lot.

Sadly, it is not unusual for experienced drivers to fail at least one component of the test more than once–I did! Even if you sail through on the first try, this can be quite an expensive endeavor. Driving school registration is usually around $300 and includes the 100€ or so to register for the test. If you pass the written test on your own, a driving school will usually let you "transfer" in for 50€. Expect to pay 30-50€ for each lesson and the actual practical test itself. At the end of the day, you'll spend at least a couple of hundred euros and more likely 500€ or more to get through the entire process. To add insult to injury, once you pass your test you will have to display the big green learner's "L" in your car's back window for a year.

Oh, the shame.

DRIVING IN SPAIN PART 2

Once you have overcome the onerous process of acquiring a license in Spain, the rest of your driving experience here is generally quite lovely and in some ways very similar to the US. There are a few differences you may need to keep in mind.

First, Spaniards pass. They pass a lot. And it has nothing to do with penis size. Passing just isn't a big deal here. Velocity is not associated with testosterone in Spain and drivers show little concern with being passed both on the highway or on local roads. On the highway, drivers keep politely to the right. Once you have passed, please follow their lead and return to the right. On one lane roads, neighbors pull to the side and wave as you pass in the opposite direction. Keep your cool. Smile.

You will find that Spain is big on traffic control and they love to use non-electric traffic cooling patterns. These are primarily one way roads, traffic circles, and speed bumps. Many of the small towns in Spain are quite old and will have extraordinarily narrow streets, so one way roads are common, but even newer areas with wider lanes may be one way.

Traffic circles in Spain are used to both keep traffic moving and slow it down. The size of circles can range from tiny in small towns to huge, multi-lane nightmare-inducing monstrosities in big cities. The challenge of traffic circles for many drivers is when following directions. Your GPS will count off the "exits" of the circle, but it isn't always clear what is an exit and what isn't. For me personally, it helps to visualize the circle as a traditional intersection. The "third exit" is often better translated in my head as "a left".

Spain has elevated speed bumps to a whole other level—pun intended. Here they are often hybrid structures that combine a raised bump and a crosswalk. Referred to as "Zebra Crossings" by many ex-pats, you will find these in most towns in the south of Spain. They come in two sizes. The narrow ones resemble the speed bumps we're used to in the US. The wider versions are literally a raised sidewalk across the road and require judicious braking to get over and past safely.

Many Americans may be surprised to find the familiar red hexagonal "STOP" signs here in Spain, but the 4-way stops ubiquitous in the US are much more rare in Spain. Instead, there are 4-way yields in many small urban intersections. Again, this is a way to keep traffic flowing, but also slow it down. The driver to your right has the right of way (unlike a traffic circle). Every driver here learns to pause as they approach an intersection. The "taxi stop" that my driver's ed teacher warned me about has found its happy home in Spain.

There are a few downsides to driving in Spain. While the main roads and highways are in excellent condition, there are many private roads here. If you are venturing off the beaten path, you will very likely find yourself on a badly paved road or even a dirt track. Although the weather is lovely 99 days out of 100...on that last day, it will rain as if the world is coming to an end. Dirt tracks are often washed out and it's not unusual for those living outside of the urbanizations to find themselves stranded for several days.

Unless you're a diehard urbanite, you may want to consider one of the small SUV style vehicles popular here. As an aside, you will find all makes of cars in Spain, from Fords to Nissans. There is a huge variety of vehicles...however, they are almost all exclusively manual transmissions. There are few automatics available and they are usually more expensive. There is also a larger percentage of diesel cars here in Spain.

Since the logistics and expenses of importing a vehicle to Spain make it not worth the trouble for most immigrants, you will most likely be buying a car here. Keep in mind that it is not a quick process and will likely take at least three days for all of the paperwork to go through. The good news is that while cars prices may be about the same as in the US, car insurance (just like home and health insurance) is much, much cheaper.

HEALTHCARE

Eight days before our flight to Spain, I fell getting into my car and ended up with a herniated disc. I couldn't walk. A lot of decisions had to be made very quickly and—as a single adult—I was the one who had to make them. Our container had already been picked up, although it had not yet set sail. Work was already scheduled for our house to get it on the market that would make it impossible to live in. I chose to go and that was one of the scariest things I have ever done. I threw myself into daily PT appointments in the little time I had left. A week later, friends walked my dogs into the airport and I was brought onto the plane in a wheelchair.

On arrival in Spain I immediately sought a physical therapist to continue my recovery. Since I didn't yet have my card for my insurance policy, the doctor's office apologized profusely for having to charge me the full private amount for a one hour physio appointment. That cost was half what my copay had been for the same exact service in the US.

As an aside, my doctor's office is not wheelchair accessible. I was walking with a cane by that point, but if not, I would have had to go to the hospital for my appointments, which was twice as far (30 mins rather than 15). There are many older buildings in Spain–as well as repurposed buildings–that are not handicap accessible. Modern buildings and buildings that have been renovated have ramps and elevators. In some cases the "accessibility" takes the form of a dangerously steep ramp built over a short staircase. Always call ahead or scout out the location ahead of time. While I was able to get up the two small steps to the doctor's office, I had to park a block away.

You could say I was thrown into the deep end of the Spanish healthcare system, and honestly, it was refreshing. The vast majority of my providers spoke English fluently and the few who didn't had already arranged for an interpreter to be waiting for me at my appointment. Our local hospital is part of the Quiron network and I have been more than impressed with the quality of the care we have received.

Since we arrived during the pandemic, the issue of vaccines came up quickly. Spain offered free vaccinations to everyone in the country quickly and efficiently. Those with private insurance were offered temporary access to the national health system and we received SIP healthcare ID cards. This put us into the national database and when our group was eligible for vaccination, we received an automatic text message with our appointment information. We were also offered flu and tetanus shots as well.

After you've been a resident of Spain for one year, you have the option of moving to the public system. Each small town or urbanization has its own health center. The number of doctors and their office hours will depend on the population the center serves. We've had limited interaction with the health centers but overall they seem to be adequate for non-emergency needs. There is a public hospital near us, but we haven't used it.

The final facet of the healthcare system in Spain is the local *farmacia*. There is a history in Spain of pharmacists dispensing a wider range of medications without a prescription than we are used to in the US. That seems to be slowly changing and more and more drugs are requiring a doctor's order here. I was thrilled to find out that I could get all of my prescriptions filled without seeing the doctor first...but then I realized that all of my doctor's visits were free anyway.

I've been able to find matches to all of the over the counter medications we kept on hand in the US. While it is convenient to be able to bring in your pill bottles and have the pharmacist give you the comparable medication, I do recommend speaking to your doctor. There are slightly different medications here and you may actually benefit from taking advantage of them. I've always preferred Ibuprofen for pain relief but was introduced to Enantyum here, which works faster at a much lower dose. The ingredient in the "PM" version of my favorite brand is available separately here so I can mix and match as needed.

I am not a health professional, but I do strongly recommend that you do your own research. Nolotil has been in the news recently as studies have shown that this common Spanish painkiller is not appropriate for light-skinned northern Europeans. Although the drug has been used by Spaniards for many years without issues, there have been multiple reports of tourists and expats having severe and often fatal reactions to it. Nolotil is banned in many countries, including the US. Doing a quick search on any medication before taking it is just a good habit to get into, no matter where you live. Doctors are human, and no one knows your (or your child's) medical history better than you do.

TAXES IN SPAIN

Many prospective expats are concerned about taxes in Spain—especially the wealth tax or solidarity tax. I am not an accountant and won't attempt to make more than broad generalizations here. The wealth tax in Spain varies between regions (and is zero in many areas) and has rather generous exemptions. I highly recommend that if taxes are a concern for you, that you find an accountant in the specific area you are considering and ask them to prepare a proforma return. This is basically a "dry run" to see what your tax obligation would be.

When evaluating tax liabilities, be sure to include in your considerations real estate taxes, healthcare expenses, utilities, insurance, and general living expenses. In addition to the thousands of dollars you're saving on healthcare, we've found all of our other expenses in Spain to be much less as well. It adds up.

Keep in mind that as a US citizen you will still have to file and pay taxes to the IRS. Sadly, the US is one of only two countries in the world that taxes its citizens when they live abroad. The good news is that there is a tax treaty with Spain which does provide some relief to expats. Consult a tax professional for details, but the oversimplified explanation is that you only have to pay one bill—although it is the higher of the two.

The important thing when it comes to taxes, is to plan ahead. Regardless of your immigration status or when your residency actually starts, you will only become a tax resident after spending 183 days in Spain within a calendar year. This is especially important if you're going to be selling your home as part of your move. The US has many tax breaks for homeowners that don't exist in the Spanish system.

As a single mom moving with a child and pets, there was no way for me to sell my home before moving to Spain. My family is not "hotel friendly". We left the US in October and I handed the keys of our home to a realtor, making it clear that my first goal was to close on the sale of our home before the end of the year, which we did.

Our fall arrival in Spain meant that we didn't have to worry about filing taxes for that year. The following year's taxes were filed the subsequent May, giving me more than a year and a half to find an accountant. Keep in mind that as an American living abroad, you have an automatic two month extension to file your US taxes, making the whole process a little more manageable.

MICHAEL OWENS

KIDS AND SCHOOLS

For the 2019-2020 school year, I enrolled my daughter in a public online school and that turned out to be one of the luckiest decisions I've ever made. Let me preface this section with the context that I am a former public school teacher and we were located in one of the best school districts in the US.

She'd had issues with bullying and I hadn't been happy with her teachers or the administration's response to my concerns so we decided to try the free online academy that is sponsored by the Virginia Department of Education. My daughter is an extrovert and, although she excelled academically, she missed seeing other kids every day. Over the holiday break at the end of 2019, she let me know that she missed in person classes and wanted to return to our local school for the following year. Then Covid hit.

We made the decision in spring of 2020 to stay with the online school for the 2020-2021 school year and that made our move a little easier. By the time we had completed our move and were settled into our permanent home it was Spring, and the end of the year was in sight. Her schoolwork for the year had all been submitted and her classes had wrapped up. Another year in the bag. Or so we thought.

One lovely spring day my daughter and I stopped by the local high school (which we could see from our back porch) to introduce ourselves and find out how to register for the coming year. We were informed quite firmly that the current year was not yet over and that my daughter could start immediately. Online school and homeschooling are both severely frowned upon in Spain. Children must be in a public school or certified private academy until they are 16. Not only does this apply to immigrants, it is a strict requirement for renewal of your visa.

We gathered all of the paperwork necessary to register her in the school—which is primarily the same paperwork needed for everything else. The school required copies of our passports, newly minted TIEs (foreigner's ID card), padrón (town resident registration), her birth certificate, a copy of her insurance card, and a photograph. You will often be asked for a NIA and a SIP card—for expats this will usually be replaced with your TIE and private insurance card. For passport pictures many of the small shops in town offer that service or there are photo booths at the mall or outside of the Carrefour. This is another instance when joining your town or neighborhood facebook groups will come in handy to find the nearest place for photos. The sizes are slightly different between ID cards and passports, etc., but the photos seem to always come in a sheet that has multiple sizes. I just hand the entire sheet to the person who requested them and they cut out the one that's the appropriate size and hand back

the rest.

So with five weeks left in the school year, my 13 year old daughter was dumped into the deep end of the Spanish education system. We had been using language apps religiously and meeting with a private tutor 2-3 times a week for over a year at that point but our Spanish was still a work in progress. In the end, she did great. And having that sneak peek of the system during the relaxed last weeks before summer was a good introduction.

While we had done research on the school system before our move, it was still all new and in some ways very different. The Spanish educational system is divided into three levels. The youngest students attend *colegios*, which correspond to grade school, roughly from age 6 to 12. Secondary schools in Spain are *institutos*. The grades from ages 13 to 16 are ESO1 through 4. Just like in the US, students must be in school until they are 16 and the completion of ESO4 is treated like high school graduation here.

It is at this point that the structures of the two systems really diverge. When teenagers in the US go off to their junior year of high school, in Spain there is a choice between multiple programs that serve as preparation for college or trade school. The college prep program is called *bachillerato* and it is further divided into science, tech, humanities, and art programs.

Language is very important in the schools here and in addition to Castilian Spanish language and literature, you will also find classes in foreign languages (English, French, Italian) and classic languages (Greek and Latin), as well as the other common languages in Spain (Catalan, Valencian, etc.). Many new arrivals are dismayed to find that their new public school teaches in the local Spanish language rather than Castilian. While our local school offered a class in Valencian, the curriculum was taught in Castilian. In addition, we were able to request (and receive) an exemption for the Valencian class. The foreign language class offered in my daughter's school was English—which she aced, of course!

In Spain, "acing" a class means getting a 10. Rather than a letter or percentage grade, students receive a number from 1 to 10 on most assignments and at the end of the year. On this scale, a 5 is passing. It is also much more acceptable than the comparable letter grade would be in the US. There seems to be far less stigma attached to a 5 than there would be to a D. While this may seem like a positive, the downside is that there is no sense of urgency or the accompanying escalation in communication that poor grades would trigger in the US. Like the rest of Europe, Spain has an excellent education system. However, the percentage of students who continue beyond the mandatory schooling age is one of the lowest in the region.

There are parent-teacher conferences each semester and grades are offered both in hardcopy and online through the parent portal, but in general I found that communication with parents was fairly rudimentary at the ESO level. The teenagers are expected to do the bulk of the work when it comes to sharing fieldtrip and deadline info, although this may vary from teacher to teacher and school to school.

PETS IN SPAIN

When I adopted my first dog from Spain in 2012, people would often ask me if I spoke Spanish. I would tell them it didn't matter, because "no" is the same in both languages. So not only does your dog already understand the most important Spanish word, they're about to become a Spanish passport holder.

Within your first few weeks in Spain, it's important to choose a local vet and take your dog in to get them registered. Note: If you have several pets, it may make sense to ask the vet to come to you. The charge for house calls in Spain is generally very reasonable. When managing several appointments, it's well worth the convenience. And even with the added home visit charge, you'll still most likely end up spending less than you would have at your old vet.

The pet registration process in Spain is two fold. You will need to register with the local government and also get an EU pet passport for your pet. My Spanish dogs already had passports, so for them we only needed to do the local registration. In the Valencian Community that system is called RIVIA. Once your dog is in the system, you will receive a credit card sized ID card for them with all of their information as well. RIVIA will

NOTE!
You may need to register your pet with your local town hall. Don't be afraid to just drop in and ask questions. They're usually pretty friendly!

also send you text messages to let you know their info has been received and when they are due for vaccinations.

The more complicated step in the process is the pet passport. If you haven't seen one of these, they look just like a human passport, but instead of documenting travel information, the pet passport has the animals identifying information, ownership data, and vaccination and health records. The most important pieces of information in the pet passport are the microchip and vaccine history.

Your dog will need to be microchipped and vaccinated before they enter Spain, but when you arrive you may need to redo these steps. In some cases, your microchip may not be compliant (especially if it is older). What is the most concerning for many pet parents, however, is that many vets will strongly recommend that you have your pet revaccinated when they receive their pet passport. Although this is not legally necessary, it is highly recommended to have an initial vaccine in the passport when it is created.

If you choose not to revaccinate your pet, you need to be very careful to carry the original USDA import permit with you when you are out and about. Since their vaccines are not registered in RIVIA, they will appear in the system as overdue. You need to be prepared to show proof of their vaccination at all times.

This is a difficult decision for most pet owners. If you have an older dog who isn't going to be outside of your home often, it may make sense to just keep their paperwork handy. If you have a younger dog that you may want to take for long walks, do dog sports with, etc. then it makes sense to revaccinate them and get their shots in the government system.

Speaking of dog sports, there are many opportunities to participate in Spain and throughout Europe. There are several dog schools where we are in the Alicante area. In addition to the regular socialization, puppy classes, basic obedience, and agility classes we're used to in the US, they also offer UK Hoopers, which is a low impact form of agility suited to pretty much any dog (and human).

Whether you're heading off to a structured class or to hang out at the local dog park (yes, Spain has those too!) or going to walk along the beach, keep in mind that all dogs must be crated or tethered while in the car. You may be fined if your dog—even a small dog— is loose in the car while you're driving. Likewise, when you arrive at your destination, please keep your pup on a leash. The fines for off-lead dogs can be surprisingly stiff here.

If your dog does get loose, you'll need to check with your local police to see which rescue your town has contracted with for stray pups. There is no municipal shelter system in Spain like we're used to in the US. In some areas there are "perreras", which function like old-fashioned dog pounds. These rarely have adoption programs. In other areas, there are charity "refuges" that take in stray pets. Each town hall contracts out the care of animals found in their jurisdiction, so it may not be the closest. It's also important to keep in mind that each region has its own rules for how long stray animals need to be held before being adopted out or euthanized. These holds can be a few days to a few weeks.

Finally, when it comes to buying food for your pets in Spain, you are in luck. There are many excellent brands available here, including all of the special diet options you're used to in the US. You can find good quality foods in your local grocery store and the larger stores like Carrefour. Your veterinarian's office and the local dog school are excellent sources for the highest quality foods.

SHOPPING

I mentioned Carrefour as a good place to look for dog food. In fact, Carrefour can be a good place to look for just about anything. Comparable to a Walmart or Target store in the US, Carrefours are large and carry everything from ice cream to underwear. They usually have a small but robust selection of English language books, a large electronics section with phones, computers, and printers, and even car care and home improvement aisles.

It's also a good place to get a man purse. Unlike most modern women, I hate carrying a bag. I have a credit card holder on my phone and a wrist strap on my keys. For the vast majority of my adult life before coming to Spain, that was all I needed. My driver's license fit in with the credit cards and I was good to go. In Spain, however, I needed to carry my passport everywhere I went for several months. Even once I had my precious TIE (foreigner's ID card), I still needed to carry my passport and International Driver's Permit until I had my actual Spanish driver's license. The little purse I bought at Carrefour came in handy during that time, but I was very happy to ditch it when I finally could.

For those from the US, Carrefour will feel very comfortable. The store setup is similar to what you will find in the US and so is the selection. Carrefour carries many US brands as well as the European brands that we're used to, such as the family of Nestle products. In the beauty section you'll find a huge array of Clairol hair colors and L'Oreal shampoos, for example.

Until emigrating from the US I never realized how many of the products I used were from other countries. My sunscreen is from Australia, my moisturizer from France, and my favorite bread is from Italy.

The other "catch-all" store that you need to know about is Merca China. Generally referred to by locals as the "Chinese Store" there are variations all over Spain. These are large buildings full of low cost options for all kinds of home goods, including furniture. There you'll find tools, bedsheets, underwear, dog collars, cookware, school supplies, and everything in between.

Beyond the Carrefours and Merca Chinas, grocery stores in Spain are somewhat smaller than what you would find in the typical suburban neighborhood in the US. You may recognize Aldi and Lidl. We prefer Mercadona and Masy Mas. Like the US, there are many different chains here, each one carrying slightly different brands. Again, American staples like Ben & Jerry's, Pringles, Doritos, Heinz Ketchup, and M&Ms are everywhere. The British grocery stores, like Overseas and Iceland, also generally carry an extended selection of American brands as well. One thing you won't often see here are the XXL containers we are used to in the US. You'd be hard-pressed to even find a gallon of milk.

In addition to the regular shops, don't discount the markets that are ubiquitous throughout Spain. Each one has its own personality, but you will generally find clothing, bed linens, fresh produce, baked goods, and—of course—the always excellent *pollo asado*. Roasted on site these chickens are juicy, tender, and flavorful. Many of the larger weekend markets have permanent stalls and include a huge variety of vendors selling everything from windows to used books. Beware that prices can vary wildly from market to market. You'll find prices higher in tourist areas.

ENGLISH IN SPAIN

Perhaps surprisingly, the one thing that you will find in most areas of Spain, and especially in the major urban areas and down along the Mediterranean coast, is English. From grocery stores to schools to the drive thru lane at McDonalds, a large portion of the population here speaks English.

Where we have settled in Alicante, English is the required second language taught in schools. As part of the Valencia region, the schools here also teach the Valencian language, which sounds to my uneducated ear like an interesting combination of Spanish (Castilian) and French. Each school's language requirements differ. In many schools there are exemptions available for Valencian by request. In Alicante, you can request an exemption based solely on the percentage of the population that speaks the language, which is low in our area.

My daughter entered the public secondary school with some trepidation. As it turns out, nearly half of her class were immigrants and most spoke English. Many were Brits, but there were also Germans, Russians, and other nationalities, all of whom spoke excellent English. Currently there are many Ukrainian refugees arriving, most of whom speak English.

Outside of the schools, you will find most people in service industries here along the coast speak at least basic English and in many cases are fully fluent. Likewise most websites for local companies and services will be available in English. If you listen to the top 40 stations on the radio, you'll find about half of the songs are from the US billboard.

The only downside to this proliferation of English is that it is incredibly difficult to find souvenirs to send to your friends and family back home. The sayings on cute mugs and t-shirts in the larger stores are almost exclusively in English—or occasionally French.

One of the major differences that I have found between the Spanish and the French is that the Spanish are thrilled if you try to speak their language. If you trot out your couple of memorized phrases they will happily switch to English with no judgement. In fact, it has become a daily personal victory if I can make it through a conversation with a Spaniard without them switching to English.

DIVERSITY

Despite the strong tradition of Catholicism in Spain, the country has no official religion and since the establishment of Spanish democracy in the 1970s it has become one of the most liberal countries in the world. During my initial research phase after my decision to leave America, I focused on legal rights of women, including the right to access healthcare. Abortion is free and legal in Spain and pregnant people as young as 16 can access abortion services without parental permission. In addition, trans men and women can legally change their gender with a surprisingly lack of bureaucratic red tape.

I had already decided on Spain and begun the visa process, when my daughter told me she was gay. I spent a sleepless night researching LGBTQ rights in Spain and what I found calmed my anxiety. In 2005, Spain was one of the first countries to extend marriage equality to its citizens. Despite Spain's notorious love of bureaucracy and red tape, the legalization of same-sex marriage was accomplished by adding one single sentence to the existing laws: "Marriage will have the same requirements and results when the two people entering into the contract are of the same sex or of different sexes." In Spain there is no "separate but equal" or "civil partnership" substitution. Marriage is the same for all couples, regardless of their gender.

As with all countries, the prejudices of the older generation may still exist—especially in more rural areas—but after living here for over two years, I have not seen it. There are rainbows, posters, and other LGBTQIA+ signs of support in public and a strong visible community where we are in the south of Spain. The major urban areas of Madrid and Barcelona, as well as the smaller cities like Murcia and Valencia, have active Queer representation as well.

As a single mother with a (queer) teenage daughter, I did not have concerns about facing sexism in Spain. After all, I had worked in tech for 25 years. In my personal experience—despite the mythos of the macho Spaniard—equality seems closer at hand here than it did at home. There may be several reasons for that. We live in a small town, but generally Spain has suffered from high unemployment for many years. Men and women alike are often willing to do whatever jobs are available. And despite those financial concerns, the people here have access to reasonable housing, inexpensive (and excellent) food, free healthcare, sunshine, and free beaches.

The quality of life here is high.

You can see the difference that access to life's necessities makes as you drive down the street. It is jarring to hear a car horn here because it is so uncommon. People don't rush through meals—and waiters don't try to hurry them along. Most people here have access to a pool or the beach.

And even the smallest bungalow usually has a walled garden. Tipping isn't a thing here, so some people find the servers rude, but in reality they just don't have to put up with your bullshit. Which means they don't go home every night and lament their lives.

Not only is everyone's quality of life higher here in the south of Spain than it was in the suburbs of Washington, DC—but there is also a sense that the people who live here understand that it isn't a zero sum game. There is a huge immigrant population where we are and the Spaniards are surprisingly welcoming. Granted, the majority of the foreigners in the larger towns are tourists who spend money, but even far outside of the tourist areas, you'll find vendors accommodating multiple languages.

Here, people have what they need, and they don't begrudge it for others. We live in the middle of farm fields and our neighbors bring us lemons, oranges, potatoes, watermelons, etc. on a regular basis.

Here, we all have enough.

VIVA LA VISA
PART 3

Ten months after your arrival in Spain, it's time to start thinking about your first visa renewal. Depending on how long it took you to get your TIE card, this may seem quite unfair, but those are the breaks. The good news is that this renewal will be for two years, so you'll get a bit of a reprieve before you have to go through this again.

In many ways, the process will mirror your visa application in the US. You do not need to request new copies of your apostilled documents, but you will need to submit them again. You will also need to provide new copies of your financial documentation.

Keep in mind that the requirements change and they always want to see a little more. If you provide documents from US banks you will need to have them translated by a certified translator and they will be closely scrutinized. Anecdotally, it seems like the foreigner's office prefers to see your financial documentation from a Spanish bank.

Up until recently, the two year renewal was a stumbling block for many retirees who were coming to Spain with savings rather than income. The Foreigner's Office was requiring those applicants to show twice as much in savings, since the renewal was for two years. For many people this was a huge burden. Ironically, those wanting to purchase permanent homes in Spain were the ones most impacted by this rule. They were torn between spending their rent money on a home versus being able to show that money in the bank...to pay rent. Fortunately it seems that most of the offices have abandoned the "double" rule and the financial requirements will be largely the same as when you applied.

If you have children under 16 on your visa, you will need to provide proof that they are in school. This is a specific document that you will need to call the school to acquire. In addition, applicants with children may also be required to submit the habitation certificate for their residence, although that seems rarely enforced.

The other documents you'll need are the same ones you have submitted previously, such as your passport, padron, birth certificates if you have children, and marriage certificates if you have a spouse. You do not need to submit the background check again at this time.

Since BREXIT, the foreigner's office in many regions has raised its standards for renewals. Applications that might have been rubber stamped two years ago are now being kicked back with very little information. If that happens to you, don't panic!

The process of renewal is very straightforward, but you can still run into trouble. We did! If that happens, reach out to a lawyer immediately. The costs to submit an appeal are usually quite reasonable, around 500€, and well worth the sense of comfort if things go wrong. If your documents are rejected or new information requested, you will usually be given ten days to comply. Do not let that time period expire without requesting an extension!

The most important thing to remember if you run into problems with your renewal is that you must not leave Spain until the issue is resolved. You will most likely not be allowed back into the country. Even if your renewal is granted, you may not be able to appear to renew your TIE—which absolutely has to be done in person. Due to an error in translation, it took six months for our renewals to be approved, which was frustrating and stressful. My only consolation was that I knew we had done everything right and it was simply a matter of wading through the bureaucratic process.

Your next renewal will again be for two years, taking your Spanish residency up to the five year mark. At that point you are eligible to apply for permanent residency.

There are two main things to keep in mind as you look toward establishing permanent residency in Spain. The first is the length of time out of the country. For each type of visa there are different limitations on how many days you can be out of Spain for both renewals and for permanent residency. Keep those in mind and plan accordingly.

The last question to answer as you approach the five year mark is whether you wish to apply for Spanish or EU permanent residency. They are similar, but the latter will give you more options to move throughout Europe in the future, if you so desire. Keep not just your own needs, but also those of your children in mind. While you may be settled in Spain, giving them more flexibility to move around as they explore colleges and careers may be beneficial.

At the ten year mark, you will have the option to consider applying for Spanish citizenship. Many Americans lose sleep over the requirement to renounce any other citizenship during the process. Please don't! Although

you may need to affirm your loyalty to your country of choice, rest assured that the bonds to your country of birth are not that easily broken.

It actually takes a great deal of effort—as well as money!—to renounce your American citizenship. It is not an easy or quick process and the steps that you take to apply for Spanish citizenship will not have any impact on your American citizenship or US passport. You can, indeed, hold two separate passports. Use your US passport to enter the US. Use your Spanish passport to enter Spain. If you are traveling elsewhere in the world, use the passport that provides the best access and protection for you and your family.

LOOKING AHEAD

As I write this we're preparing to submit our second renewal, which will take us to the five year mark and permanent residency. Was Spain exactly as I imagined? No. That was the dream—this is the reality. And I love it. At the end of the day, I think every part, every step, was a little more work than I expected it to be. But the results are well worth it.

Am I fluent in Spanish? Nope. I don't know if I'll ever be completely fluent, but I can get around pretty well and I continue to see progress with my language skills. I've been considering an intensive language course in nearby Alicante to bump me up to the next level and that may be in my near future.

I left the US in 2020 because I couldn't see a way forward, even under the best case scenario.

For the most part, I think that's what we've had. The US is on much better footing today, as far as the international community is concerned...and yet women and queer Americans have lost rights, and continue to do so. The judicial branch has been poisoned so thoroughly by the GOP's underhanded dealings, that it will take a generation to recover. In the meantime Americans will suffer.

If you don't have a passport, get one. Today. Prioritize taking trips abroad to find a place that you and your family will be safe and comfortable. Travel can be expensive—but there are deals available if you can be flexible. I've flown roundtrip from New York to Madrid for under $400. The train here is cheap and there is a full range of accommodations from hostels to campgrounds for the frugal traveler.

For recent college grads— or not-so-recent—there are "Auxiliares de Conversación" programs specifically designed to bring Americans to Spain to teach English in schools. These usually involve about 20 hours of work a week and in return you will receive a visa and a stipend of about 1000€ a month. These are similar to student visas, which are also a great option at any age.

My point is...come. Visit. Take a long weekend or stay for a month. You have options, you just need to reach out and grab them.

MICHAEL OWENS

ABOUT THE AUTHOR

A member of Gen X, Michael Owens was born to two people who should never have had children. Her mother thought it would be cool to give her daughter a boy's name. Her father's only contribution was the genetic gift of height. As a 6ft tall woman named Michael, this introvert has never had the option to fade quietly into the background. Accepted as a 15-year-old to Johns Hopkins University, Michael went on to complete four degrees. She has been a teacher, an artist, and a web designer (and other fancier titles that mean web designer) and founded a rescue that has saved over 1000 dogs. In her early 30s Michael abandoned the dating world to become a single mother by choice via artificial insemination. Thirteen years later her daughter, Augusta, completed her first novel, The Hummingbird Coven. Inspired by her precocious teenager, Michael dusted off a story she had started in the previous millennium and turned it into her first published novel, *The Windless Sky*.

Today Michael and Augusta live in the south of Spain, saving dogs and writing books.

BY MICHAEL OWENS

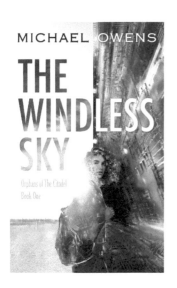

Fulfilling her mother's dying wish, Maisy goes to live with her estranged father on the Citadel, a fancy name for an ore processing plant built into the side of an asteroid. There she discovers the terrible truth…space is boring. No alien princesses, no cool cyborgs. Just a greedy corporation that controls everything from the food you eat to the air you breathe.

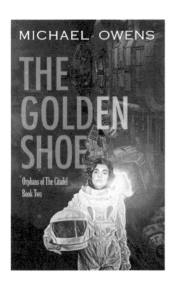

Maisy and her friends have been expelled from the Citadel. Now they're limping their way toward a newly discovered planet aboard the Golden Shoe, a "colony ship" that is nothing more than a badly damaged freighter held together with duct tape and good intentions. But they soon learn that they aren't alone out here.

Made in United States
Troutdale, OR
09/23/2024

23079567R00066